The Sunflower

Steve April

The Sunflower
ISBN 13: 978-0-9744686-3-1

c/o POB 4475
Mountain View, CA 94040-0331

A Barberry Book
Printed in the U.S.A.

will the sunflower turn to us, will the clematis…
— T.S. Eliot

You were never no Locomotive, Sunflower, you were a Sunflower!
— Allen Ginsberg

A "tiny golden human form of the Sunflower, with petal-like arm, root-like leg, and hair flowing back…"
— William Blake

to Maxine

Contents

1

Great pines balancing
White moon, silver clouds,
Love's gymnastics visible.

Poem of life,
Did Photon make it back,
The guardrails tell no lies.

Cries so sweet and urgent,
Branchhoppers, grasshoppers,
My ears are exploding.

High beams stronger and stronger
Search the darkness,
And darkness stronger too.

One more image before I go
The two of us hand in hand
On Fire Mountain.

The night enveloped me
I sat on a silver rail,
A star dropped.

Starry dynamo
More than a privileged witness,
Through you most I.

I am a child of light
And a child of darkness,
Empire West our estate.

Rejuvenation at dusk
A fountain of youth,
Or simply your voice.

Happy 4th graders,
In Grand Union,
Meeting of meat and divinity.

For love complete
One must knock,
The other open the door.

Laughing, unmasked
My master Shakespeare
Fills my car with joy and triumph.

The startled deer grazing
On the lawn
In the rear view mirror settled down.

Full moon over the speed bumps
And exit signs,
Cool, indifferent, remote.

Lucky chance on a mountain road
The deer in my headlights
Let me pass.

Big mountain, big sky
A great accepting feeling
In the air.

Where was I yesterday,
Where will I be tomorrow?
Ask the mountain.

I would adore heaven and earth
With my song
Under the witness tree.

Even if divinity can be seized
For a moment,
Where is it heading?

What would you ask of the men?
Can the counsel of sand
Catch the wind?

I call down the summer moon
Call down the sun,
Your faithful servant calls.

Ask no more questions
Give in to the night
Let it carry you away.

Durable stuff
This vessel,
Between a myth of longing and regret.

Coming down off the mountain
The air changed, grew heavy
Magic is local.

Every moment, every waking hour
I am
Making my confession.

The breeze dies in the elms
Morning,
The night uses me as a vessel.

2

Sky and earth meet
At the horizon, grand union
Double your pleasure.

High flying bird
What is great soon falls,
Mountain pine I love you.

Artists are carriers
Many-colored messengers,
Feast and famine sing.

Poet consumed
Your burn-out is your badge
Your love a funeral pyre.

Arise speckled bird, arise
Reborn from your ashes
New missions arise.

Keep me safe and sound
Music and world beat,
Other rhythms pass by.

What will be will be
Even if my suitcase is gone
Let them take it.

They stand at my shoulder
Cold group of eager ghosts
Superego let go.

I call down the rain
To drown their music,
A storm to wash them away.

The sky tonight
Ghost-rider of another time and place,
Not one bird.

Way down the feeling comes
By Golden's Bridge,
Losing battle, winning war.

Mr. Coffee, Mr. Waters
A styrofoam cup is rolling
Down a hill.

Sun sets down like a rocket
A flourish of trumpets,
Dusk blazes golden.

Good night, sleep tight creation
No no, not yet
Not with the lights on.

Do not curse your enemies
Water and fire oppose
And complement.

Big orange sun on the horizon
Who dare frame and sing
Harmonize.

This majesty, this beauty
It breaks my heart,
Forgive this dance, teacher.

Spell out Nature's beauty
In an alphabet of pearl
I will learn it.

All paths look the same
From the top of the mountain,
Each top different.

Bells on the hill
Just to keep that image,
As dusk washed them silver.

On a tough journey
Where the slope is slick and rough,
Simplify.

This fair kingdom, this bountiful estate
Surrender,
Perish the thought.

Tremendous evening
Reap and sow
If this be the crop, so be it.

Auld Lang Syne,
The divinity made me cry
Never say goodbye.

Star-spangled nightfall
This sunset my banner,
Ticket to paradise.

To the ceremony of divinity
Human form divine,
Immortals guide me.

Sermons of stone yield
Come seasons of forgiveness,
Baptismal springs.

Who could suffer my charity?
The snake sheds his skin
And moves on.

Fireflies flicker on high rocks,
Darkness falls
Like a window.

Nowhere to run but backward,
Backward into your arms,
And the future.

As one passes away another appears,
Journey is endless
As my mind.

No more communions or consummations
Tender night grows weary,
Relent.

3

Now forever always happy 5th babe
One star
Over the pine trees.

In this trance of Indian summer
Even crickets
Repeat themselves.

Could that be a waitress
Crying for her lover?
Just a slumping pine.

The night is so still, nothing comes
Silence swells
Until a car sweeps by.

The I apart, distinct, remembers all
His journey
Through creation.

4

Something beautiful is dying
Autumn crowns
The valley below.

Light from the houses
In the valley,
Twinkling, shimmering like stars.

Vision of promise
Valley below,
Misty rain on my face and hair.

This is my loving kingdom
Rainy night, bright future
Crickets sing on.

Big trees awash in the sky's tears
Bowing like children,
Guardrails fade out.

The great rains, the greater promise
Feed me, drown me
Let it come down.

A shooting star like a flare
I am pregnant,
I am the carrier.

Lion and lamb my coat of arms
Look Milton I bear
A kind message.

This autumn I am swimming
In an Indian summer
Star-coat secure.

No star above, no Northern light,
Eager navigator
Still happy.

In jeopardy any moment
Here at the great divide
Ceres, forgive me.

As if I were a thief
In the rain I confessed
I pleaded guilty.

Mystery of mysteries
Down by the reservoir
In a star-coat.

Though I am a heedless mortal
Ceres forgave me
And blessed me.

5

Toward the end of the millennium
The weather
Got much warmer.

A bluebird launches itself
From a high bough,
Dusk settles silver.

Ever ancient, ever youthful mountain
House of mysteries,
Deer runs.

Chariots of fire
Draw closer,
By the millennium thundering.

Melting snows, flowing waters,
Acres of dead wood
Evoke the carnage.

A breathless pause
Dusk draws in,
Giant leaf tumbles down the highway.

Creatures great and small
Open their eyes,
In high nests and low tunnels.

Ceres' immense machinery
Is put in motion,
Pit and pendulum.

Too early yet for revelry,
This shuffling,
This shedding of skin.

Budding beauty
The mighty sun discloses,
Part of larger flowering.

Even if there is nowhere to go
And no one to be,
Let it flow on.

Tender buds disclose,
It is your time
Time of tearing thrills, ambitions.

All for love and lust,
You begin your journey,
Day's journey to rending.

Hestia, vestal virgin
Rough strife ahead,
Prepare them for their journey.

Even if my feet remain cold
Mountain trees softly sigh
Moriah.

Flowing and still
Solid and yielding,
Reconcile your opposites.

Return and enter
Tender trespasser,
Husband this garden and sing.

Vessel open and ready
In this strong breeze,
Lithe gods flow through my limbs.

All mine until the sun
Is blown out like a candle,
Magic circle.

Limber day, tender night,
Privileged witness
Unite them, untie them.

Inspire me, heal me
On your mountain, in your glades,
Bells are ringing.

Just when all was abandoned
All was scattered,
A clarion call.

A touch of magic,
A touch of grace,
Like a big finger in the sky.

Life is a pile of vials
Between two smiles,
And dials for miles.

Just when spring seemed to announce
The sky goes white,
The flower closes.

Presumptuous child
Playing on this ship,
Like Photon at home on the bridge.

Circus Maximus, this spring day
Altar like for Venus,
And Ceres.

Some part imagination,
Some part desire and strife,
Our bigtop cafe.

What could I ask, Gods
That has not been given,
The gift is complete.

This beauty, this miracle of desire,
Trees swell with it,
So do I.

6

Gaining more control
Of the darkness,
Season of forgiveness and triumph.

My battery failed
But still I felt good
Romancing the mountain.

Out of the darkness, two strangers
In a car
Helpful angels.

They gave me a jump
And followed me down
Then headed to Buffalo.

Each person special, unique
In mid-journey,
Jostling each other.

If you lose it no-one can use it
Billboard proclaims
Out the window, red bridge.

Tour of busty boughs
And telephone lines,
Train ride through a volcano.

Risk and reward go hand in hand
Like rose and thorn,
Train and 3rd rail.

Clean buildings, clean streets
Below the surface
Mortgages, assignments, suits.

Lost in Yonkers,
The dedicated rider
And the wide-eyed adolescent.

Green valleys and hills
Brave little graveyards
Summer afternoon rolls by.

The most unlikely, the most abused way
My road to greatness,
Have faith.

Immense lobby, streaming thousands
Grand Central
Dim frescoes on the roof.

History and mystery come together
Two guys from Phili
Pass.

She strolls in
Without a care in the world
My beautiful comrade.

Her hair like a rainforest
Thick enough to get lost in,
Sometimes I do.

My strength, this lies in my sameness
Drama playing through me,
Unfolding.

Fixations, obsessions
Drop, leave them behind
But where is the future?

Backdraft,
This is my letter to the world
That sometimes turned with me.

Echoes of darkness life after life
Promising bells,
Haunted heartlands.

Woman gazing at a sign
Innocent upturned face,
White blossom.

Myth of fingerprints,
Myth of victim,
What will substitute in their place?

Young and old alike
Lope, saunter through this watering hole
Grand Central.

Our very appearance in the world
Raises questions,
Dark horse on a dark course.

Lions, tigers and bears
Roam the dark wood,
Dante and Dorothy meet.

I stepped into an avalanche
That covered my soul
My lucky day.

Traders are smoked
Blaze closes annex,
A transformer exploded.

Later, smell the life
The wild pussy blossoms
Wafting in the air.

Take the blood in my veins
Make it solid and lasting,
Shape of a heart.

Starry, starry night
Over our commute train
Heading to White Plains.

Grief tore him limb from limb
As he floated down a river
He spied Eurydice.

Her strange birth-condition
Wore sun-glasses for many years
Had many operations.

One eye matches another
Almost perfectly,
A friend of a friend.

So much left to do
And so little time
Desperation like bear-fangs.

A soul thirsts for renewal
For a living god
Stations pass quickly.

My wealth, virtues, strength
Flower in relation,
Gorgeous mosaic.

Going by the iron-works,
These rails my teacher,
Comes Fordham station.

A bomb with a ribbon around it
That was Frieda's phrase
Package deal.

An artist is a switch
Playing mad, not mad
Alternating currents.

Hold the wavelength
Relation with the heavens
What else has this value?

Orion, Hercules,
Bright stars in the heavens,
Guide, defend us.

Lacking soil to grow in,
Lacking roots or water,
Simulated culture.

Trees waving in the wild breeze
Sun crowning a hill,
Capture me with emotion.

Kafka, king of rain,
Blake and Whitman magnifique
Shakespeare, tender king.

Wavy trees, pink twilight
Around the gritty tracks,
Sunflowers triumph.

Swell mystery
Easy to talk to,
Like having coffee with a friend.

What angels keep the sanity quotient
Stable
Touched with devotion?

My poor heart yearns for God,
Sense of divine, source of renewal,
Future.

Are angels on the lam
Apprentices among us
Earning their wings?

Do they at last transform
Into something more dazzling,
Colossal?

That someone as beautiful as you
Loves, values me,
Incredible.

Holmes triumphant
All the crime in London
Caused by Moriarty.

The weather today
Shaking peacock feathers,
Some Indian summer.

You are my fulsome beauty
Scope and path,
Only the heavens fathom.

Sweet emotion touched with devotion
My song,
Your fanfare and prayer.

No escaping, no changing my imperative
Do or die
Poet.

With an outpouring of salt and sweat
She rides me
A very goddess.

Alabaster love calls
And outside girls of summer
Flip their shades.

To tell a story, leave a record
My mission
Here in record time.

When stars collide
Pisces, Ares and so on, scatter
In all directions.

I am more handicapped than you
Therefore have a heart,
Bring me to you.

To deal fairly with childhoods
And the sea,
Play in it not with it.

Take Shakespeare's royalty
Through Ovid's changes, Conrad's
Storms, our journey.

When the sea's roar sounds like a woman
An odyssey
Is upon you.

As we mortgage our future to a tin man
Heavy metal
Plays on.

Everything is mysterious
Then revealed in a flash
Painful planet.

Our will brings us to our own expression,
What we enjoy
Bears fruit.

The look in that child's eye
A mute animal
Charging with wisdom.

The green boy from space
Found a sister
In Grand Central and Westchester.

All nations, all territories
Seek reunion
With the world.

Through the lighted windows, curtains
How much beauty, desire
Behold.

Rainy night in New York City
Cabs by the river
In battalions.

Guardian of dreams, visions
Door-man
In a New York city high-rise.

Where the chimes of freedom
Meet the dark dirty waters
Loose the cannon.

He lived like it was
Last night on earth,
Trustee of desire and childhood.

Diego Rivera,
Your world so sensual,
So radical.

Marcuse liked sensual pictures,
Dreamland escapades
Liberating.

Shaman escapades
Conquer your fears,
Let yourself be overrun.

Hear other voices
Different rhythms,
Forming a circle of life.

Clasp to your naked bosom
In great fraternity
This wheel of life.

Collisions, smashing, crashing
Hierarchy of impulses
Dissolving.

Greyhound in the Mt. Laurel station
Window, inside out,
Upside down.

Vacant lots, shabby highrise,
Crossing Walt Whitman bridge
Into Camden.

7

In this wonderland
Gravest danger
Craving for extreme sensation.

Shell, Ramada, Burger King,
Bars and cars,
American century.

On platform dancing
To the Pointer Sisters
Drunk as skunks, law school party.

Back to the heart of the matter
Where I loved and loved you,
Tears fall like rain.

Privileged witness, envoy
What is your assignment,
Do you need lodging?

From stars they come, light beings
Blake's angels
Who kindle, fan our embers.

There we go in times of trouble,
Nestling at our own light core
Revealed.

Do not desert me sacred visitor
My door is open,
Come in.

Is she in one piece
Or scattered wide like Orpheus?
News, please tell me.

Only a divine interpretation
Can help her
Doctors divine.

Moon is bright maiden light
Yours is the promise, yours the gifts
I attend.

Your beauty and style
The way you give
The way it is supposed to be.

Beautiful mermaid, bountiful mermaid
Your time is coming
To shine.

A heart made for joy
A mind alive,
The world is richer for you.

Regarding children I am an optimist,
Adults
I am puzzled.

Sweet smell of success
Good work, good love
Truly the daily double.

As a guardian, trustee
To protect, love the children
Our future.

Today Jim Bakker
Apologized for using God
To gain wealth.

Sat on the mountain
As the red-ball sun set
Listened to Grateful Dead.

The mountain is great
Was here before me, will be here after
Salute.

Breezes from around the world
Caress me, entice me
Invite me.

Sacred place, power place
Ceremonies of innocent love
Greetings.

Can feel the youths who had visions here
Who fasted here,
Rites of passage.

The gods meet here, their spot too
Magic place, magic time
With sacred rules.

Only to be freed of the earth
To nest on a leafy bough
Then fly off.

Buffalo, antelope, ponies,
Pow wows in the tepee,
Then the hunt.

Though not a native
The mountain an offering
I cannot refuse.

Here the air is clear
Here the breeze is strong
A great Spirit moves here.

The State as a hungry animal
That just keeps growing
Wanting more.

This wide big breeze blowing through me
Commends me to
The mystery dance.

Vista from Deer Run Road
Pastures of plenty on and on
To twilight.

By Sondak farm the strawberries
In the pink twilight
Were inviting.

Minnewaska Park in the evening,
Lone camper
In a vacant lot.

Crickets sing, breezes ruffle the small
Trees, leaves seem to dance
On the skyline.

Dignified, sturdy, loyal
If trees could fight
What good soldiers they would be.

Crickets grow louder by the minute,
Mandolin wind
Tunes the mountain.

Why even go back
Here all is forgotten, forgiven
Mountain rules.

A speck on a ball
Is a lonesome rider,
Can do little damage.

I give my devotions to some mystery
Rivers, valleys,
Mountains.

Vessels of peril, midway
Between a past and a future
Blueprint.

Vessels of peril on the lam
Need to pray
To touch the dynamo.

A great breeze whips leaves
Into a fury
As car roars down the mountain.

Summer sat with us
Lazy, contented
After she leaves we miss her.

Soon hills and sky will merge
And shadows run from themselves
To the darkness.

Waiting for a sign
From the divine mind
My part in this passion-play.

Be a juncture where rivers meet,
A crossroad for highways
Changeling.

Boy prophet there
At the meeting place of two seas
Where are you heading?

My faith flows from my nature
Great night I am for you
Mountain, hold me.

Where sea meets land
Where sky meets earth
In contradiction, I abide.

Contradiction is an echo
But unity is there
Homecoming.

A toy for divinity, their rattle
This be your balm
Not alone.

Youthful are the gods
The longer they reign, younger they are
Baby-talk.

Well-connected circuit, musical chairs,
Starlight electric
My source.

Eagle scouts learn to tie knots
Policemen radio,
I too make connections.

Down from a great height
Up from a great depth,
Colossal powers converge here.

Are we alone?
Whose is the body we turn to,
Walk on as dawn breaks?

A mystery keeps bobbing out of reach
Like a buoy
In deep water.

I be a faithful servant
Errand boy for mystery,
Am ready.

Orange moon over the treetops
Followed me down the mountain,
Numinous.

Lovely valley all at peace
Green valley at peace,
Muted music.

Paused by Briggs Highway
For air,
Night enfolding me like a lover.

When your mind is troubled
Listen to your heart
It will not desert you.

An unfulfilled longing
More like a dream
Holds me in my deep heart's core.

Agamemnon for his kingdom
Would do anything,
Too bad for you.

Balance of mighty forces,
Blade of grass and star,
Wonder of nature.

Thanks is my attitude
Awestruck witness,
Hands together in prayer.

Purple mountain
Ribbons of corn fields
Sun ending its gallop, going down.

What have we gotten into
Through double door?
Our continuing mystery.

Like yesterday
Standing on the lawn writing,
"Rich as the air we breathe."

The life of a leaf,
The life of a tree, eternal,
Sensational.

Only to carry messages
Do errands,
Across the universe.

Tokens of a better time,
Grandeur with a crown,
Came back to jog me.

www.ingramcontent.com/pod-product-compliance
Lightning Source LLC
LaVergne TN
LVHW050944080826
845145LV00004B/1402